The Seamless Robe

Brian Johnson

First Printed 2016

Copy printed by REFRESHMENT UK
156 Waterloo Road, Blackpool, Lancashire FY4 2AF
Registered Charity 1153542

British Library Cataloguing in Publication Data
A catalogue record for this book is available from the British Library

ISBN 0-9931641-5-6

Cover design & Typeset by Simon Cooper

Photo taken by Brian Johnson

Contents

Preface

There may be some points in this book that challenge you. If that causes you to be like the people from Berea in Acts 17; "examining the scriptures daily to see whether these things were so." Then I have achieved my object, even if you don't agree with me.

The Word of God is living and active which is why I not only write about it, but quote and include chunks of it in my books.

I have received encouragement and support from many whom I wish to thank, especially from my wife Gill. I also wish to thank Lindsey Thompson, just when I think it's perfect she ploughs her red proof reading pen through it all correcting my mistakes.

At the end of each chapter, there are some questions which will help you reflect and enable you to do further Bible Study.

Comments

What did this book do for me?

It made me scamper back to the Scriptures, search out certain readings and question, 'How on earth had I never seen that myself before?' Certain parts reaffirmed that which I already understood, whilst others gave me completely fresh insight into the Word.

It made me thankful that the Lord we serve was obedient to our Father and fulfilled every requirement so that I, a sinner, can go boldly before my Abba Father and know that in Him I have received full forgiveness.

I know Jesus is our Great High Priest, I know He is from the tribe of Judah, so why did I never question the fact that priests were always from the tribe of Levi? Thank you Brian for opening my eyes and deepening my understanding through this study.
Linda Allitt (Active Member of Coton Green Church).

Wow!! I have never thought of it like that before. Thank you Brian for opening up this subject in a new and unique way. The concept of Jesus being a High Priest in the Order of Melchizedek has always been a mystery to me but after reading this it is a mystery no longer. It all makes perfect sense.

Come on let's put on the seamless robe and strive to do all that Christ wants us to do and be all that he wants us to be. What an honour it is to be Christ's representatives on earth. How can we not be determined to serve Him with all our hearts.
Thelma Cameron (Active Member of Coton Green Church).

Another useful booklet in the series. The concept of the seamless robe is made a fascinating one both in personal experience to the author and the biblical exposition of the wider insights into the person and ongoing ministry of Jesus. The concluding challenge to the see the diverse yet unbroken nature of the universal church is a vital issue today.
Dr Richard Massey, Former principal of Birmingham Christian College.

I really enjoyed Brian's latest book 'The Seamless Robe'. To me, this was more of a bible study, and as a more mature Christian, something I could get my teeth into. I especially enjoyed the section on Melchizedek. In the bible high priests and kings were different people with different roles, but Brian articulated really well how Jesus has taken on both roles, by being both our great High Priest who is able to intercede with God for us and forgive our sins, and also our Lord and King whom we should revere, worship and serve.

The Seamless Robe' portrays how, if we are willing to submit to Him, we can be woven into the fabric of His love and service, and become part of the family of God.
Lindsey Thompson
Lighthouse and Teenage Group Co-ordinator Coton Green Church.

Brian's little books are full of insight and inspiration from the Holy Spirit. He brings a wealth of Bible knowledge and mature Christian faith to everything he writes. In the 'Seamless Robe', I was quite blown away by the revelation about the High Priest Caiaphas – that when he tore his robe during Jesus' trial before the Sanhedrin he was prophetically ending the old Levitical priesthood and acknowledging that Jesus is our High Priest in the order of Melchizedek, as the book of Hebrews teaches.
Annie Routley. Christian Music Ministries.

INTRODUCTION

I saw a white *seamless robe* lying on the ground.

In those waking moments when you drift from sleeping to a wakeful reality, I saw a picture in my mind of the empty cross of Christ. Then as I looked down to the foot of the cross, I saw a white seamless robe lying on the ground. The picture focused my attention and I was soon wide awake. "What is the meaning of this, Lord?" I thought through the surrounding events at the time of the Crucifixion as laid out in the Gospels. I was hoping this would help me discover what the Lord was saying.

Matt 27:51-53 ... and behold, the veil of the temple was torn in two from top to bottom; and the earth shook and the rocks were split. The tombs were opened, and many bodies of the saints who had fallen asleep were raised; and coming out of the tombs after His resurrection they entered the holy city and appeared to many.

Some non-scriptural writings state that the "veil" was a patchwork quilt and about four (some say eighteen) inches thick! It was torn from top to bottom, but this delicate seamless robe lay at the foot of the cross unharmed.

This delicate seamless robe lay at the foot of the cross unharmed.

Ps 22:18 ... they divide my garments among them, and for my clothing they cast lots.

This was prophesied a thousand years earlier and confirmed by a witness (St John) who said:

John 19:23-24 Then the soldiers, when they had crucified Jesus, took His outer garments and made four parts, a part to every soldier and also the tunic; now the tunic was seamless, woven in one piece.

(Some translations say woven from top to bottom). 24 So they said to one another, "Let us not tear it, but cast lots for it, to decide whose it shall be"; this was to fulfil the Scripture: "They divided MY outer garments among them, and for MY clothing they cast lots."

What was the significance of this Seamless Robe? Why had the Lord brought it to my attention? It was a Sunday morning. Maybe I should share about it at Church but, nothing opened up in the morning and so I was still none the wiser by lunch time. In the afternoon, I had been invited to a short retreat. There were about twenty-five people there and none of us knew more than two or three others. After a while, my old cynical nature reared its ugly head and I began to think, "What a rag tag bunch we have here, a real patchwork quilt."

> "My church is not a patchwork quilt but a seamless robe."

The afternoon passed quickly and, after dinner, we all went to the chapel. It was a time of prayer and worship which was beautiful. I began to think, "They're not such a bad bunch; these are my brothers and sisters who love the Lord as I do." Then the Holy Spirit reminded me of my earlier thoughts and the Lord said, "My church is not a patchwork quilt. This "rag tag bunch", which you are part of, is a Seamless Robe that I am weaving from top to bottom. I have woven you into the robe and anyone that you bring to me, I will also weave in. You can watch as each thread is seamlessly added." Wow! What was that again? "My church is not a patchwork quilt."

According to the World Christian Encyclopaedia there are at least 33,000 different denominations or Christian groups worldwide varying in doctrine and churchmanship which to me sounds like one massive patchwork quilt!

Yet as far as Christ is concerned, it's a Seamless Robe! He prays to the Father for His disciples.

John 17:22- 25 … the glory which you have given me I have given to them, **that they may be one, just as we are one;** I in them and you in me, that **they may be perfected in unity,** so that the world may know that you sent me, and loved them, even as you have loved me. Father, I desire that they also, whom you have given me, be with me where I am, so that they may see my glory which you have given me, for you loved me before the foundation of the world.

Here is an interesting point to bear in mind for later: at this time Jesus would have been about thirty-three years old, yet He says to the Father, "you loved Me before the foundation of the world." This shows that He existed before the world's foundation. Other scriptures convey that the Father and Son were one and co-existed before the foundation of the world

The world sees the different Christian groups as a patchwork quilt, and from the outside looking in, I would agree; yet in the Lord's eyes, it's a Seamless Robe. Yes, it is showing diversity but also having unity, being one with each other and the Lord. Just as the Trinity is three different persons in one Godhead so Christians, although spread over 33,000 denominations, are all part of One Church.

It is the glory of Christ in each of us that makes us ONE, not the name plate on the church door or our churchmanship. Paul said in Col 1:27 Christ in you the hope of Glory.

There is a lot more to this seamless robe.

However, there is a lot more to this Seamless Robe as I found researching the topic. What about the robe itself? What was it? Was it a common garment? The soldiers didn't want to tear it - not that they consciously wanted to fulfil scripture as they were Romans and would not be familiar with Hebrew scripture. They knew it was valuable and so would hope to sell it for profit. Apparently, in the whole Roman Empire, Israel was the only place where they could be purchased.

A complex looming system was needed to make one, which only the Israelites understood. The most common group of people to wear them was the temple priests. Not every priest had one **but the high priest most certainly would have worn one** when executing his priestly duty. So why was Jesus wearing one? He was a rabbi from the tribe of Judea; only the tribe of Levi could be priests. The more I looked into it, the more I discovered. If priests could only be from the tribe of Levi, why, in the book of Hebrews, does it refer to Jesus as a priest.

> Heb 7:17 "You are a priest forever according to the order of Melchizedek."

> According to the order of Melchizedek

The key to the reason is in the word "order". The existing priests had been operating under the "Levitical order" set up by Moses with Aaron and his sons who were all from the tribe of Levi. Suddenly they came to the end of their era, something happened which made them redundant. They had been in power for over 1300 years but instantly something changed the "order". One seemingly small event changed the course of His story.

QUESTIONS

1. In the vision what was at the foot of the cross?
2. What was prophetically protected and by which Psalm?
3. According to the World Christian Encyclopaedia how many different denominations are there worldwide?
4. What did Christ pray for in John 17:22-25?
5. Which group of people would be the most likely to wear the Seamless Robe?
6. Out of that group who would most definitely be wearing it?
7. Which were the two "orders" mentioned?

CHAPTER ONE
ACCORDING TO THE "ORDER OF MELCHIZEDEK"

So who was this guy Melchizedek? I've discovered he goes way back, in fact so far back it gives a clue as to who he might be. The name Melchizedek means King of Righteousness. So he was a king, also a priest, and also King of Salem, which means peace and is where Jerusalem gets its name, city-peace. There was another complication: He (capital H) was and is eternal and does not have any genealogy. By which it does not mean the records were lost but that there was no-one before Him, because He always was, and no one to follow Him because He never dies and always is.

Heb 7:1-3 For this Melchizedek, king of Salem, priest of the Most High God, who met Abraham as he was returning from the slaughter of the kings and blessed him, 2 to whom also Abraham apportioned a tenth part of all the spoils, was first of all, by the translation of his name, king of righteousness, and then also king of Salem, which is king of peace. 3 Without father, without mother, without genealogy, having neither beginning of days nor end of life, but made like the Son of God, he remains a priest perpetually.

Oh dear, we have a problem. Not just righteous (good) but the king of righteousness (goodness). Now when the rich young ruler came to Jesus, He said, referring to Himself, "There is only One who is good (righteous)."

> There was no one before Him.

Matt 19:16-17 ...and someone came to Him and said, "Teacher, what good thing shall I do that I may obtain eternal life?" 17 And He said to him, "Why are you asking Me about what is good? There is only One who is good."

Let's think about an equation; to be accurate it has to balance; it has to add up. So on one side we have, the king of righteousness + someone with no beginning and no end + the king of peace + being like the Son of God.

On the other side let's try ~~ordinary human beings.~~ No, that won't work, we are born and die and are not that good (righteous) anyway. What about ~~angels?~~ No, they were created beings. How about ~~the Devil?~~ No, he is a created being, plus Melchizedek was a good guy, blessing Abraham after he defeated the evil, robbing kings. The Devil wouldn't want to bless him for that! I think all we are left with is a form of God, and we will try to show which person in the Trinity Melchizedek is.

Every Christmas season a very popular scripture is sung:

> Isa 9:6-7 For a child will be born to us, a son will be given to us; and the government will rest on His shoulders; and His name will be called Wonderful Counsellor, Mighty God, Eternal Father, Prince of Peace. There will be no end to the increase of His government or of peace, on the throne of David and over his kingdom, to establish it and to uphold it with justice and righteousness from then on and forevermore.

We have some overlap here. In Hebrews 7, it talks about Melchizedek being king of peace and righteousness, also like the Son of God. Here in Isaiah, the prophecy uses the same titles referring to peace and righteousness, also about the coming Christ child referring to Him as a Son.

The Bible gives people names with meanings and often more than one name, so don't be confused by so many names referring to the same person. A child is born but a Son is given. So the Son must have existed before the child was born as we saw when Jesus mentioned that the Father loved Him before the foundation of the world.

Matt 1:23 Behold, the virgin shall be with child and shall bear a Son, and they shall call His name Immanuel," which translated means, "God with us."

The child became a man but had God in Him.

The child became a man but had God in Him. Or, more accurately, the person of the Son of God became a human child who grew into manhood. He was God but limited Himself to being human.

John the Baptist talking of Jesus said,

John 1:15 "This was He of whom I said, 'He who comes after me has a higher rank than I, for **He existed before me'."**

That's strange John, elsewhere in Scripture it says you were born six months before Jesus. Oh, you mean that He existed before He was born as the man Jesus!

You are not yet fifty years old, and have You seen Abraham?

How about when Jesus was talking to the crowds.

John 8:56-59 "Your father Abraham rejoiced to see My day, and he saw it and was glad." 57 So the Jews said to Him, "You are not yet fifty years old, and have You seen Abraham?"

58 Jesus said to them, "Truly, truly, I say to you, before Abraham was born, I AM." 59 Therefore they picked up stones to throw at Him, but Jesus hid Himself and went out of the temple.

How much plainer did He have to say it? Could the day that Abraham saw and rejoiced be when He appeared to him as Melchizedek?

There are a number of accounts in the Bible of a "special person" appearing to different people throughout history. Many theologians believe this "special person" to be Christ. Theophany is the theological term for these appearances. Literally it means a manifestation or appearance of God to a person. Let's look at some cases of theophany to build up the picture.

One like an angel of God appeared to her...

We will start with the story of Samson. His mother was barren and "one like an angel of God" appeared to her and prophesied that she would have a child. Her husband wanted to meet this "Angel" and check it out. So he prayed and the "Angel" appeared.

Judges 13:15-23 Then Manoah said to the angel of the Lord, "Please let us detain you so that we may prepare a young goat for you." 16 The angel of the Lord said to Manoah, "Though you detain me, I will not eat your food, but if you prepare a burnt offering, then offer it to the Lord." For Manoah did not know that he was the angel of the Lord. 17 Manoah said to the angel of the Lord, " What is your name, so that when your words come to pass, we may honour you?" 18 But the angel of the Lord said to him, "Why do you ask my name, seeing it is **wonderful?**" 19 So Manoah took the young goat with the grain offering and offered it on the rock to the Lord, and He performed wonders while Manoah and his wife looked on. 20 For it came about when the flame went up from the altar toward heaven, that the angel of the Lord ascended in the flame of the altar. When Manoah and his wife saw this, they fell on their faces to the ground. 21 Now the angel of the Lord did not appear to Manoah or his wife again. Then Manoah knew that he was the angel of the Lord. 22 So Manoah said to his wife, "We will surely die, **for we have seen God**."

23 But his wife said to him, "If the Lord had desired to kill us, He would not have accepted a burnt offering and a grain offering from our hands, nor would He have shown us all these things, nor would He have let us hear things like this at this time."

The scripture we looked at earlier in Isaiah 9 says, and His name will be called **Wonderful** Counsellor, Mighty God, which includes the same word "Wonderful" in Hebrew that the "Angel" used when He appeared to Manoah.

> And His name will be called Wonderful Counsellor, Mighty God,

Now consider Joshua. Moses had just died and it was left to Joshua to lead the people into the Promised Land. Then he has this confrontation.

Joshua 5:13-15 Now it came about when Joshua was by Jericho, that he lifted up his eyes and looked, and behold, a man was standing opposite him with his sword drawn in his hand, and Joshua went to him and said to him, "Are you for us or for our adversaries?" 14 He said, "No; rather I indeed come now as captain of the host of the Lord." And Joshua fell on his face to the earth, and bowed down, and said to him, "What has my lord to say to his servant?" 15 The captain of the Lord's host said to Joshua, **"Remove your sandals from your feet, for the place where you are standing is holy."** And Joshua did so.

Two things stand out to me: first when Joshua bowed down in an act of worship he was not told to stop as John had been when he bowed before an angel.

(Rev 22:8-9 I fell down to worship at the feet of the angel who showed me these things.

9 But he said to me, "Do not do that. I am a fellow servant of yours and of your brethren the prophets and of those who heed the words of this book. Worship God".)

Second point: although Joshua bowed down, the Lord would have known his heart and recognised he was possibly not totally realising who was addressing him. So the Lord told him to remove his sandals because he was on holy ground.

This was also said to Joshua's boss Moses when the Lord appeared to him in the burning bush.

Exo 3;2-6 The angel of the Lord appeared to him in a blazing fire from the midst of a bush; and he looked, and behold, the bush was burning with fire, yet the bush was not consumed. 3 So Moses said, "I must turn aside now and see this marvellous sight, why the bush is not burned up." 4 When the Lord saw that he turned aside to look, God called to him from the midst of the bush and said, "Moses, Moses!" And he said, "Here I am." 5 Then He said, "Do not come near here**; remove your sandals from your feet, for the place on which you are standing is holy ground**." 6 He said also, "I am the God of your father, the God of Abraham, the God of Isaac, and the God of Jacob." Then Moses hid his face, for he was afraid **to look at God.**

Then there is the night Jacob wrestled with a "man" all night.

Gen 32:29-30 Then Jacob asked him and said, "Please tell me your name." But he said, "Why is it that you ask my name?" And he blessed him there. 30 So Jacob named the place Peniel, for he said, "I have seen God face to face, yet my life has been preserved."

> "Please tell me your name."

Either Jacob was mistaken or the man was God in human form, which again points to another manifestation of Christ before the birth of Jesus.

One manifestation may be doubtful but a number (and there are more) tend to show that God has always made connections with His people, with any who seriously seek Him.

So in Christ, or *as* Christ, Melchizedek established an order which started well before the Levitical priesthood. So what was the, "small event that changed the course of His story"?

QUESTIONS

1. Why can't Melchizedek be seen as an ordinary human priest?
2. How can John the Baptist say Jesus existed before him if the man Jesus is six months younger than John?
3. What does Isaiah say about a son being born?
4. What name is given to the common manifestation experience of Jacob, Joshua and Samson's parents?
5. Why did the crowd want to stone Jesus when He said Abraham was glad to see His day?
6. Why did the angel stop John from worshiping him?
7. Why did the manifestation that appeared to Jacob, Joshua and Samson's parents accept worship if only God should be worshipped?

CHAPTER TWO
THE SEAMLESS ROBE THAT WAS TORN

So, again I ask, "What was the small event that changed the course of His story?" For more than a thousand years the Hebrew Scriptures predicted the coming of the Messiah, or in Greek, the Christ. This would be someone who already had an amazing CV before coming to Earth in human form; a person who would defeat the Israelites enemies and be their king.

Yet there were other prophecies of a humble person, one who would heal the sick and give His life for their sins and be their High Priest pleading before God on their behalf. Not everybody saw the overlapping prophecies or realised that they were actually one and the same person.

There was an occasion when Jesus and His disciples visited Caesarea Philippi, a town steeped in Greek and Roman religions with shrines to their gods. These gods included Pan, the god of the wild and shepherds with their flocks. This may have given rise to Jesus teaching elsewhere, "I AM the good shepherd". inferring Pan was not. It was here that Jesus asked His disciples what people were saying about Him.

> "You are the Christ, the Son of the living God."

Matt 16:13 -17 Now when Jesus came into the district of Caesarea Philippi, He was asking His disciples, "Who do people say that the Son of Man is?" 14 And they said, "Some say John the Baptist; and others, Elijah; but still others, Jeremiah, or one of the prophets." 15 He said to them, "But who do you say that I am?" 16 Simon Peter answered, "**You are the Christ, the Son of the living God.**" 17 And Jesus said to him, "Blessed are you, Simon Barjona, because flesh and blood did not reveal this to you, but My Father who is in heaven."

Could it be that Peter saw the shrines to Pan and remembered what Jesus had said earlier and realised who He was?

Over a three-year period Jesus made a massive impact on the nation. People were healed and delivered from unclean spirits; some of the people repented and the disciples baptised them. All of the people were amazed at the authority He had; and yet there were undercurrents, particularly amongst the leaders. These events came to a climax during the Passover celebrations. The temple authorities had Him arrested and brought before the Sanhedrin, some of whom, including Caiaphas, were Sadducees. They were the aristocrats and did not believe in the afterlife, the prophecies about a Messiah or the resurrection.

Enter the humble Carpenter-Rabbi-Messiah.

Imagine a court house with all the officials in their robes looking very serious. Also lined up were some citizens prepared to be false witnesses against Jesus. Enter the humble Carpenter-Rabbi-Messiah. Caiaphas the High Priest challenges Jesus,

> Matt 26:63-65 "I adjure You by the living God, that You tell us whether You are the Christ, the Son of God." 64 Jesus said to him, "You have said it yourself; nevertheless, I tell you, hereafter you will see the Son of Man sitting at the right hand of Power, and coming on the clouds of heaven."

Unless you are familiar with Scripture you wouldn't realise the significance of what Jesus said. In His answer He quoted from Psalm 110 which is all about the coming Messiah, and that the Messiah was also a priest after the order of Melchizedek (not after the "order" of the Levitical priesthood). This was an in-your-face declaration that left no doubt in the minds of the leaders that He was confirming Himself to be the Messiah and Son of the living God.

That provoked Caiaphas, (even though as a Sadducee he did not believe in the Messianic prophecies) to do something that would end the Levitical priesthood.

65 Then the high priest **tore his robes** and said, “He has blasphemed! What further need do we have of witnesses? Behold, you have now heard the blasphemy; 66 what do you think?” They answered, “He deserves death!”

Caiaphas tore his clothes!

Caiaphas tore his clothes! Under absolutely *no* circumstances is a priest, and particularly a High Priest, allowed to do this. At the very least the punishment was that he could no longer remain as priest, and at worst it meant death.

Lev 21:10 'The priest who is the highest among his brothers, on whose head the anointing oil has been poured and who has been consecrated to wear the garments, shall not uncover his head **nor tear his clothes.**

So the seamless robe of Caiaphas was torn. There stood before him a priest of a different order, not from the tribe of Levi, wearing a Seamless Robe that was not torn.

Heb 7:17 “You are a priest forever according to the order of Melchizedek.”

Jesus is now the official High Priest

Jesus is now the official High Priest, not by His own instigation but by that of His Father's. It is His duty to take the sacrificial lamb atoning for the sins of the people into the presence of the Most High God. He is both priest …and sacrifice. Just as Isaac carried the wood to the place of sacrifice for his father Abraham, so Jesus carried the wooden cross to the place of sacrifice.

At the last minute God provided a lamb for Abraham so Isaac was saved, but Jesus was "The Lamb of God"; He *was* the sacrifice. After the crucifixion, His body was taken away but the Seamless Robe lay at the side of the cross, untorn as an eternal witness to His priesthood and to Him being the sacrificial Lamb of God.

Unaware of the significance of Caiaphas' torn robe, the temple officials continued with their ritual of the Passover. This centred around the sacrificial offering of a lamb being slain and the blood offered up on the altar. Then a scapegoat had the sins of the people symbolically laid upon its back and then the goat is led out into the wilderness. Historically the goat never returned which was confirmation to the people that their sins had been forgiven and wiped out. But apparently the goat came back...five times!

Another tradition the Jews had was to tie a crimson thread of wool on the sanctuary door. By evening it would miraculously turn white as a sign that their sins were forgiven. On this occasion and for the next forty years (until the temple was destroyed by the Romans) the thread stayed crimson.

Some believe that the scripture in Isaiah 1:18 confirms this tradition.

> "Come now, and let us reason together," Says the Lord,
> "Though your sins are as scarlet, they will be as white as snow;
> Though they are red like crimson, they will be like wool."

> The thread stayed crimson

Since that time, (when the temple was destroyed) the ritual has not been performed with sacrifices. There is neither temple nor need because there is a priest, after the order of Melchizedek, who took the sacrifice before God Almighty and pleads day and night on our behalf.

So does the order of Melchizedek take over? Do they both run side by side, or does one of them take control.

QUESTIONS

1. Whom did Peter recognise Jesus as?
2. Why were there undercurrents among the leaders?
3. What did Caiaphas do to be excluded from the priesthood?
4. Who followed Caiaphas as High Priest and why?
5. Why did the goat come back?
6. What made Caiaphas lose his temper?
7. As the new High Priest what did Jesus take and offer as a satisfactory sacrifice?

CHAPTER THREE
LEVITICAL AND MELCHIZEDEK ORDERS?

We know that Abraham met with Melchizedek. This is recorded fourteen generations after Abraham by King David in Psalm 110. Then twenty-eight generations later Jesus quotes David. There are about 430 years between Abraham and Moses then another 600 years to David.

> Abraham met with Melchizedek

Moses set up the Levitical priesthood which lasted until just after Christ, that was about 1300 years. Yet in the middle of that period David (in Psalm 110) is talking about Melchizedek as though He was an existing superior priest to which he paralleled his Lord.

> Psalm 110:1-4 "Sit at My right hand until I make Your enemies a footstool for Your feet." The Lord will stretch forth Your strong sceptre from Zion, saying, "Rule in the midst of Your enemies." Your people will volunteer freely in the day of Your power; in holy array, from the womb of the dawn, Your youth are to You as the dew. The Lord has sworn and will not change His mind, "You are a priest forever according to the order of Melchizedek."

If Melchizedek was spiritually active 600 years before Moses introduced the Levitical priesthood, why did we need the Levitical priesthood? For us to understand that, we need to look at some more history. When Moses delivered the people of Israel from slavery out of Egypt and led them to the Promised Land they could have been there within three months. Instead it took them forty years. Why? Moses sent spies to survey the land and they come back with a report.

> Numbers 13:25-27. When they returned from spying out the land, at the end of forty days,

26 they proceeded to come to Moses and Aaron and to all the congregation of the sons of Israel in the wilderness of Paran, at Kadesh; and they brought back word to them and to all the congregation and showed them the fruit of the land. 27 Thus they told him, and said, "We went in to the land where you sent us; and it certainly does flow with milk and honey, and this is its fruit."

So far so good; the report about the land was excellent. So what was the problem?

Numbers 13:28-29. "Nevertheless, the people who live in the land are strong, and the cities are fortified and very large; and moreover, we saw the descendants of Anak there. 29 Amalek is living in the land of the Negev and the Hittites and the Jebusites and the Amorites are living in the hill country, and the Canaanites are living by the sea and by the side of the Jordan."

Uh-oh! Can you see what's coming? Some of them are preparing to express their fears but Caleb interjects.

Uh-oh! Can you see what's coming?

Numbers 13:30-32. Then Caleb quieted the people before Moses and said, "We should by all means go up and take possession of it, for we will surely overcome it." 31 But the men who had gone up with him said, "We are not able to go up against the people, for they are too strong for us." 32 So they gave out to the sons of Israel a bad report of the land which they had spied out, saying, "The land through which we have gone, in spying it out, is a land that devours its inhabitants; and **all the people whom we saw in it are men of great size."**

There are earlier biblical references to giants and the spies believed they had seen their descendants.

However, we won't go into that just now. It took forty days to spy out the land then after their report the people refused to enter the land. Sadly, they spent the next forty years in the wilderness. God provided and took care of them but they did not trust or want to get too close to God. His glory and power frightened them. The adult generation that refused to enter the land all died in the wilderness except Caleb and Joshua. According to Jewish records and dates this act of disobedience happened on the 9th of Av. This is the same date as a list of tragedies in Jewish history including the destruction of the first temple, and the temple in 70AD; the crusades, the expulsion of Jews from England, France, Spain and the start of the Holocaust in 1941. This is just to mention a few, but back to the plot.

They did not trust or want to get too close to God

Looking back to the days of the patriarchs the head of the family acted as a priest praying for those in his care. See Job 1:4-5

His sons used to go and hold a feast in the house of each one on his day, and they would send and invite their three sisters to eat and drink with them. When the days of feasting had completed their cycle, Job would send and consecrate them, rising up early in the morning and offering burnt offerings according to the number of them all;

For Job said, "Perhaps my sons have sinned and cursed God in their hearts." Thus Job did continually.

God's plan, when Moses led the people of Israel out of Egypt, was to make the Israelites a nation of priests to all nations.

Exo 19:5-6. Now then, if you will indeed **obey** My voice and **keep** My covenant, then you shall be My own possession among all the peoples, for all the earth is Mine; and you shall be to Me a kingdom of priests and a holy nation.

However, because of sin they broke the covenant (the law) with God losing their right to be a priestly nation and instead He decided to make one tribe priests to intercede for all the people. That group was the tribe of Levi. However, it seems they weren't ready to even be priests over their own families never mind the nations. So the time was not yet right for a priest after the order of Melchizedek to emerge. They had been four hundred years in slavery and sadly could not take that step of faith which would have been the beginning of a new lifestyle. Instead of embracing a relationship individually with God they told Moses to speak to God on their behalf.

> Instead of embracing a relationship individually with God they told Moses to speak to God on their behalf

Deut 5:24:27 'Behold, the Lord our God has shown us His glory and His greatness, and we have heard His voice from the midst of the fire; we have seen today that God speaks with man, yet he lives. 25 Now then why should we die? For this great fire will consume us; if we hear the voice of the Lord our God any longer, then we will die. 26 For who is there of all flesh who has heard the voice of the living God speaking from the midst of the fire, as we have, and lived? 27 Go near and hear all that the Lord our God says; then speak to us all that the Lord our God speaks to you, and we will hear and do it. '

Even though Moses reported what God said, they did not obey. In fact, all the law did was to expose our human inability to fully keep it, (only with Christ in us is that possible); so the "thou shalt nots" became "I cannot". The Levitical priesthood taught the law which was perfect in every way, but it had no mercy. It was all about cause and effect. Step in front of an oncoming train, you get utterly smashed. There is no mercy, no excuse, no, "I didn't see it coming". If you stand on a railway line, when the train comes the result is death: cause and effect.

> The "thou shalt nots" became "I cannot"

John 1:17 For the Law was given through Moses; grace and truth were realized through Jesus Christ.

The grace that was to come can only be found in and through a priest after the order of Melchizedek, not a priest after the order of Levi. Jesus did not do away with the law but fulfilled it, (satisfied its demands on our behalf).

When law was given and the people sinned by worshipping the golden calf, 3000 people died. After Jesus paid for our sin and grace was released and preached on the day of Pentecost, 3000 people repented and were saved.

They did not die but were given eternal life. Jesus was a priest after the order of Melchizedek, who is the King of Righteousness, therefore righteousness was imputed to the repentant.

QUESTIONS

1. How long did the Levitical priesthood last?
2. How many days did the spies survey the land for?
3. How many years did they wander in the wilderness?
4. All who refused to enter the land died in the wilderness except the two men who advocated going in. Who were they?
5. What was God's original plan for the children of Israel when He set them free from Egypt?
6. What was God's Plan B and how long did it last?
7. When did Plan B end and the new order begin?
8. What was the name of the priesthood other than that of Melchizedek?

CHAPTER FOUR
KING OF SHALOM

Melchizedek was the King of Shalom (peace). The English word, "peace" can just mean the absence of conflict or war. Shalom is more comprehensive than just peace. It means so much more than that. It includes wholeness, completeness, prosperity (spiritually, mentally and physically), peace, and harmony. That is why it is such a wonderful greeting and blessing when you meet and leave a friend to say, "Shalom".

As I said before, Jerusalem means the "city of peace" and Melchizedek was the King of it. When He came out to the King's Valley and met Abraham (Gen 14) He not only blessed him but brought bread and wine: bread to sustain him and wine to refresh. When the King of Shalom comes to you, it is not to condemn you because you have broken the law but to bless you with forgiveness, wholeness, completeness, also to sustain and refresh you.

If you receive Him, like Abraham did, He can do all this because He is not only the King of Shalom but also of Righteousness. That is the very meaning and essence of His name. This means He has the power to impute His Righteousness into those who will receive and trust Him.

> Rom 4:3 For what does the Scripture say? "Abraham **believed** God, and it was credited to him as righteousness."

So it is not by "fully obeying" the law (**which none of us can do) that makes us righteous but by believing or "fully trusting**" in God, as Abraham did, that credits us with righteousness.

> Isa 61:10 I will rejoice greatly in the Lord, my soul will exult in my God; for He has clothed me with garments of salvation, He has wrapped me with a robe of righteousness.

Just as the father of the prodigal gave His son a beautiful cloak on his return, Melchizedek gave Abraham, in spiritual terms, a robe of righteousness. I believe it was seamless, not a patchwork quilt, and it enveloped him completely with no gap in its protection; all because Abraham trusted God.

Just as Melchizedek came out to bless Abraham, giving him bread and wine after the battle; now, in the person of Jesus, He comes to us. Not as a Levitical priest, because only by fully obeying the law without one slip, or act of imperfection can we be made righteous through the law. However, God made the impossible possible by sending Jesus to pay for our sin and then impute His righteousness to us as soon as we accept what He has done for us.

> But according to the power of an indestructible life ...

Heb 7:11 Now if perfection was (possible) through the Levitical priesthood (for on the basis of it the people received the Law), what further need was there for another priest to arise according to the order of Melchizedek, and not be designated according to the order of Aaron? 12 For when the priesthood is changed, of necessity there takes place a change of law also. 13 For the one concerning whom these things are spoken belongs to another tribe, from which no one has officiated at the altar. 14 For it is evident that our Lord was descended from Judah, a tribe with reference to which Moses spoke nothing concerning priests. 15 And this is clearer still, if another priest arises according to the likeness of Melchizedek, 16 who has become such not on the basis of a law of physical requirement, but according to the power of an indestructible life. 17 For it is attested of Him, "You are A priest forever according to the order of Melchizedek."

So let us accept the biblical teaching that when Jesus went to the cross and died for us He set aside (made redundant) the Levitical priesthood and became our King and High Priest forever.

Now Plan A can take effect. No longer do we need the sacrificing of animals. No longer is it only the High Priest that goes through the veil once a year. Now the old veil is torn so that all who have accepted Jesus as Saviour and High Priest can enter the Holy of Holies, the presence of God!

Exo 19:6. ...and you shall be to Me a kingdom of priests and a holy nation.

A kingdom of priests and a holy nation. A royal priesthood

This is not replacement theology (teaching that the Church replaces the nation of Israel). More than that, all Jews or Non-Jews who accept Jesus, become part of God's nation. Peter refers to people who are not "a people" becoming "a people" and even more, "a royal priesthood".

None of the kings came from the tribe of Levi; only the tribe of Judah. Jesus was from the tribe of Judah and from the line of King David both on Mary and Joseph's blood line. However, because Jesus did not have Joseph's blood but the Heavenly Father's, the curse on Joseph's line (Jer 22:30) was bypassed and the promise of Gen 49:10 was fulfilled.

Jesus was also a priest after the order of Melchizedek. Therefore, the head of a Royal Priesthood! This could not have happened from the Levitical priesthood.

1 Pet 2:9-10 But you are A chosen race, A royal priesthood, A holy nation, A people for God's own possession, so that you may proclaim the excellences of Him who has called you out of darkness into His marvellous light; 10 for you once were not A people, but now you are the people of God; you had not received mercy, but now you have received mercy.

The writings of the New Testament show clearly that they were written for people with Jewish and non-Jewish cultural backgrounds which I will show in the next chapter.

QUESTIONS

1. What were the two areas that Melchizedek was king over?
2. On what grounds was Abraham considered righteous?
3. How can someone be considered to be a priest after the order of Melchizedek?
4. Give a full understanding of the word "Shalom".
5. What is God's Plan "A"?
6. What is replacement theology?
7. How did the Levitical and Melchizedek priesthoods differ?

CHAPTER FIVE
THE WORD OF GOD

When John wrote his gospel, he used wording that cut right across different cultural back grounds. Any living language changes, words change, meanings change. A simple example would be the word "cool". Years ago it meant a temperature between warm and freezing. Now it means something that impresses.

> Dead languages do not change but still talk

Fortunately, the Bible is written in two dead languages. The meanings remain the same, they do not change. When composing the writer has to choose words that will convey information in an understandable manner. Nevertheless, no matter how good the writer is, we are still left needing to know what was in the heart and mind of the writer. That is where the Holy Spirit comes in - to give us clarity and revelation. He not only inspired the writer back then but is also our teacher now.

This next section shows examples of how words are understood in different ways by different cultures. Also the interesting numerical characteristics found in the bible based on the number seven. It is like God's watermark to prove the Scriptures are not just writings of men but inspired by Him. In many sections, patterns based on seven turn up. For instance, Psalm 110 which we have already looked at, has a total of 63 Hebrew words (7 x 9). There are a further 13 different features in this psalm all based on number seven. The probability of this just happening is seven multiplied by itself 14 times which is 1 in 678,223,072,849. Now that is just in one small section of scripture! The whole Bible is saturated with similar patterns.

Now let us look at a small section in John 1:1-2,

> In the beginning was the Word, and the Word was with God, and the Word was God.

2 He was in the beginning with God... 14 And the Word became flesh *(a man)*, and dwelt among us, and we saw His glory.

Later the scripture reveals that this Word that became a man was actually Jesus. Now John was a Hebrew - speaking Jew, but he was writing with the Jew, the Greek *and* us in mind. How did he do that?

Well, the Greek word for "Word" is "Logos" which is an expression in Greek philosophy. In part it means "the total expression" of something or "the rational principle that governs and develops the universe". So to the Greek, it reads something like John 1:1-2.

In the beginning was "the total expression", the rational principle that governs and develops the universe and the "total expression" was with God, and the "total expression" was God. 2 He was in the beginning with God... 14 and the "total expression and rational principle that governs and develops the universe" became flesh *(a man)*, and dwelt among us, and we saw His glory, (and that man was Jesus).

Wow! John in his opening comments had completely cut right to the core of the Greek mind set. If the Greek accepted John's opening comments from that point on, all that John said would be accepted by the Greek. John had taken an 'up in the clouds', airy, philosophical expression and replaced it with life and a real person.

So that met with the Greek; how about the Jew?

John 1:1-2, In the beginning was the Word, and the Word was with God, and the Word was God. 2 He was in the beginning with God... 14 And the Word became flesh *(a man)*, and dwelt among us, and we saw His glory.

The Hebrew boy, by the time he was thirteen, knew the first five books of the Old Testament off by heart! As soon as John said, In the beginning the Jew would think of the same opening words in the book of Genesis describing creation. Then the next part, was the Word, and the Word was with God. Ah yes the Word of God! To the Jew he knew from Scripture that God created everything from nothing by His spoken Word. God said, "Let there be light" and instantly, there was light coming out of God's mouth at 186,000 miles per second, but what would the remaining part make him think? And the Word was God. 2 He was in the beginning with God... 14 and the Word became flesh *(a man)*, and dwelt among us, and we saw His glory. Now his brain was in overdrive! Yes, eventually a Messiah would come but if this is true then Jesus was and is the Messiah! This time John had reached the Jew, he touched a sensitive nerve. If Jesus was the Messiah, then he needed to hear what else John had to say.

> Now his brain was in overdrive

But how did John also have us in mind? We have lived for centuries in a land that has a Christian culture. Although not all are believers, most have gleaned some of the basics. Most would know there is a God and that Jesus Christ was sent as a man who said some amazing things and performed miracles. So when we read, John 1:1-2.

> We have lived for centuries in a land that has a Christian culture.

In the beginning was the Word, and the Word was with God, and the Word was God. 2 He was in the beginning with God... 14 And the Word became flesh *(a man)*, and dwelt among us, and we saw His glory.

(And that man was Jesus) We think what on earth is this "Word" he's talking about? Then we see that this "Word" is Jesus. Oh now this fills a few gaps.

It makes a real link to God through the person of Jesus. For many this interesting start would prompt them to read more of John's gospel.

This chapter is entitled, "The Word was God" to conclude there is another aspect in this section I didn't include earlier.

> John 1:2-5 He was in the beginning with God. 3 All things came into being through Him, and apart from Him nothing came into being that has come into being. 4 In Him was life, and the life was the Light of men. 5 The Light shines in the darkness, and the darkness did not comprehend it.

We are still talking about this Word that was with God and was God! It is hard to grasp that this humble blue collar carpenter they crucified on a false charge of blasphemy was the engineer creator of EVERYTHING! He is also the light of the world that could shine through us. Although here the Scripture says He is the light of the world, elsewhere He refers to US as being the light. A group of young children were asked what a saint was. One bright young girl said, "He is someone the light shines through". When asked to explain what she meant she said, "Well when you go into a church with stained glass windows some have pictures of saints and the light shines through them".

> He is someone the light shines through

We have no light of ourselves; like the stained glass window we need "The Light" to shine through us. The light shines through the Word giving us revelation, but the Word, which is active, generates the light in the first place. God spoke the Word, "let there be light".

Rather like the conundrum, which came first, the chicken or the egg, which came first the Word or the light?

QUESTIONS

1. What are the advantages of scripture being written in dead languages?
2. How did John relate to the Greek mind set in John chapter 1?
3. How did John relate to the Hebrew mind set in John chapter 1?
4. How did John relate to our mind set in John chapter 1?
5. What else is Jesus referred to as well as the Word?
6. What do we have in common with the stained glass window?
7. How did God create light?

CHAPTER SIX
BACK TO THE SEAMLESS ROBE

After all it was just an article of clothing

So what else can we learn from the Seamless Robe? Why did scripture prophesy about its protection? Why was it protected? After all it was just an article of clothing, wasn't it?

God wants us to seek Him; He drops clues to encourage us, to reveal greater depths and layers of truth. Each layer builds a platform from which we can reach higher into the knowledge and mind of Christ

I would often tease my children in conversation to provoke them to think. Silly conversations like, "Daddy I'm hungry." Hello hungry." "I'm not HUNGRY!" "Oh, I thought you said you were hungry!" After a while they learnt to think how to express their thoughts so that I couldn't mess with them. Or they would say something to try and trick me. All of this helped to develop their minds.

Likewise, He wants to interact with us, have conversations. We come to love and trust Him through His involvement in our lives. So we say, "Lord, I'll do whatever you want me to do". He says, "OK, but what would **you** like to do?" He wants to work with us because He sees us primarily as family, not as servants. God created us in His own image. He has free will. So do we. He could have programmed us like a computer but He didn't.

The creation account reveals something of God's nature. A phrase often repeated states whatever He created should reproduce, "each after its kind" So if He created us in His own image He wants us to be His children and to grow up like Him, the creator designer, accepting Him as Father of us all.

Whilst there is some flexibility within a species' development nevertheless a cow doesn't become a horse; nor does a monkey become a human being. So what can we learn from the Seamless Robe?

There are many fulfilled prophecies about Christ's life. Maybe the Seamless Robe was just another fulfilled prophecy to make up the numbers. No, I think there must be more to it than that. I have found with my Father, He reveals layer upon layer of truths and, the more we see of those layers, the closer we get to His heart. He wants us to sit with Him, (see my book, "Come sit with Me") to fellowship with Him, to interact with Him. I used to sit with my children at bedtime and tell them a story. "Did I ever tell you about the time…?" They loved it and so did I. Our Father is just the same. Let's think about this Robe, mulling over in our minds what we can learn, what is relevant for us today.

The robe was not left in the holy chambers

Referring to the priests, Ezekiel said they had to wear linen garments next to their skin (like the seamless robe) when entering the Inner Court of the Temple. Jesus, unbeknown to the others, fulfilling His Father's will, was prepared to take up the role of High Priest when brought before the Sanhedrin in the Inner Court for trial. He did not say, "OK guys, I'm taking charge now. Move over".

No, He was appointed by His Father.

Heb 7:17 "You are a priest forever according to the order of Melchizedek".

(Read the whole of Hebrews 7 for a fuller picture.) So He needed to wear the Seamless Robe to both spiritually and physically declare that He was a High Priest even though He was from the tribe of Judah. This was further proof that the Levitical priesthood was over.

Why else would a different priest of a different order need to enter the temple if the Levitical priesthood was still in power?

Ez 44:17 It shall be that when they (the priests) enter at the gates of the inner court, they shall be clothed with linen garments.

Later when Jesus went to the cross, the robe was removed. This would comply with Ezekiel 44:19.

When they go out into the outer court, into the outer court to the people, they shall put off their garments in which they have been ministering and lay them in the holy chambers; then they shall put on other garments so that they will not transmit holiness to the people with their garments.

Another layer of truth confirmed. “Ah!” I hear you say. “But the robe was not left in the holy chambers.” You have a point but the Sanhedrin was not aware that He was a priest of a different order. To the upper class dignitaries of the Sanhedrin, He was just a blue collar carpenter. He, however, was of an order that wanted to transmit holiness to the people. He was a priest who moved among lepers; laying hands on them for their healing. This was an act completely against their culture. The lesser Levitical system required holy things to be kept separate in case unholy items polluted the holy. Now, through the new order, the holiness was stronger and would make holy whatever it came in contact with, not the other way round.

There was also a risk (under the Levitical order) that the unholy person could die if they touched something holy because they did not have righteousness imputed to them. There is another point. Aaron had to wear the priestly clothes, when ministering, as a shield so he did not take on the guilt or sins of the people. The whole point of Jesus going to the cross was to take on Himself our guilt and die for us.

That is another reason for the garment being removed at the cross, to remove the shield, and conversely it being left for us to wear (spiritually) as a shield, when we minister to others with sin in their lives.

Ex 28:43 They (the priestly clothes) shall be on Aaron and on his sons when they enter the tent of meeting, or when they approach the altar to minister in the holy place, **so that they do not incur guilt and die**. It shall be a statute forever to him and to his descendants after him.

Although completely human, because He was filled with the Holy Spirit, His holiness was greater than any un-holiness that may try to pollute Him. Hence He had the ability to touch lepers and not be infected. This power is granted to those who follow Him in discipleship and are filled with the Holy Spirit.

In My name they will cast out demons

Mark 16:17 These signs will accompany those who have believed: in My name they will cast out demons, they will speak with new tongues; 18 they will pick up serpents, and if they drink any deadly poison, it will not hurt them; they will lay hands on the sick, and they will recover.

I will also redeem you with an outstretched arm and with great judgments.

There are four cups of wine ceremonially drunk at the Passover meal celebrating God's deliverance of Israel from slavery in Egypt. On the night of the last supper, they did not drink the final cup. The four **"I will"** statements in the scripture below are each toasted separately throughout the meal. The third one, **'I will** also redeem you with an outstretched arm and with great judgments', was to be fulfilled by Christ as He took upon Himself great judgments with outstretched arms for our sin and thereby redeeming us. This is the cup we drink at communion.

Ex 6:6-8 Say, therefore, to the sons of Israel, 'I am the Lord, and **I will** bring you out from under the burdens of the Egyptians, and **I will** deliver you from their bondage. **I will** also redeem you with an outstretched arm and with great judgments. Then I will take you for My people, and **I will** be your God; and you shall know that I am the Lord your God, who brought you out from under the burdens of the Egyptians. And I will bring you in unto the land, concerning which I lifted up My hand to give it to Abraham, to Isaac and to Jacob; and I will give it you for a heritage: I am the LORD.'

The fourth cup was to celebrate their inheriting the Promised Land after being redeemed, set free and escaping from their captures. That is why Christ did not drink the fourth cup at supper because, until He went to the cross, they were still not fully redeemed.

Mark 14:25 Truly I say to you, I will never again drink of the fruit of the vine until that day when I drink it new in the kingdom of God.

It was on the cross that the fourth cup was given. The time that Jesus drank the wine on the cross coincided with the exact time the priests were performing the Passover sacrifice in the temple.

When the time was right on the cross, He drank the last cup.

John 19:28-30 After this, Jesus, knowing that **all things** had already been accomplished, to fulfil the Scripture, said, "I am thirsty". A jar full of sour wine was standing there; so they put a sponge full of the sour wine upon a branch of hyssop and brought it up to His mouth. Therefore, when Jesus had received the sour wine, He said, "**It is finished**!" And He bowed His head and gave up His spirit.

> It is finished! Nothing missed out, all prophecies fulfilled!

It is finished! The price has been paid! Mankind has been redeemed! Nothing missed out. All prophecies fulfilled. The High Priest after the order of Melchizedek drank from the fourth cup to celebrate the victory, died and spiritually passed the priestly robe on to His followers that they may become a nation of priests. This may conjure up in your mind all of us walking around wearing a robe and sandals or a dark suit and a dog collar. You may be feeling that this is not you. What we will be wearing *physically* is irrelevant; *spiritually* we will be wearing ALL that is of Christ!

There are a number of roles we are asked to play. How about the role of Ambassador?

> 2 Cor 5:20 Therefore, we are ambassadors for Christ, as though God were making an appeal through us; we beg you on behalf of Christ, be reconciled to God. He made Him who knew no sin to be sin on our behalf, so that we might become the righteousness of God in Him.

The role of ambassador is to represent his nation within another nation. We are citizens of Heaven but, here on Earth, we represent Christ. As priests and ambassadors, we minister the new covenant of grace and salvation to the world around us. Although we live in the world our heart's desire is to see the world transformed into the Kingdom of God. This is not just for Christian leaders but for all Christians to have the life of Christ pouring through them.

Next we will look at what part and power the Seamless Robe plays in our lives. Are we ready to spiritually wear the robe and take up the role He has given us?

Rev 5:10 “Worthy are You to take the book and to break its seals; for You were slain, and purchased for God with Your blood men from every tribe and tongue and people and nation. **“You have made them to be a kingdom and priests to our God;** and they will reign upon the earth.”

Now is the time for Plan A to take effect. A people in relationship with God bringing holiness and the knowledge of salvation to neighbours and nations alike.

QUESTIONS

1. Why did scripture prophesy about the seamless robe?
2. Are we created in the image of God with or without free will?
3. If creation was designed to reproduce “after its kind” where does that place the theory of evolution?
4. Did Jesus self-appoint Himself as high priest or was He appointed by another?
5. Who appointed Jesus as high priest?
6. How many cups of wine are ceremonially drunk at the Passover meal?
7. When did Jesus drink the last cup?

CHAPTER SEVEN
PLAN A

Finally, now Plan A can take effect. Finally, God's plan to reach the world with His love and mercy can be mobilised. Finally, it will be realised He saved Mankind from the deceptive lies of Satan who perverts the law of God to condemn us.

I often wonder what Moses did for those forty years looking after Jethro's sheep in the wilderness.

I often wonder what Moses did for those forty years looking after Jethro's sheep in the wilderness. He had been through the Egyptian education system for princes. Did he have a PhD in classical literature and languages? King David as a boy looking after sheep wrote and sang psalms. Did Moses start to put together some of the first five books of the Bible that he wrote? Or did he not start that until the time of wandering around the wilderness with the twelve tribes of Israel? We do know he completed them before he died when Joshua took command.

Moses, Joshua and Caleb must have been immensely disappointed with the people who were afraid to enter into the Promised Land. They missed God's Plan A, (that the people be a nation of priests as we saw earlier). Now instead of everyone being guided by the Spirit of God, they were under the law; but the law had no mercy. If you are walking a tightrope without a net and you manage to walk all the way to within a couple of feet of the other side before falling, you still fall the same as the person who fell after just managing a couple feet from the start. Keeping most of the law cannot justify or save you any more than someone who hardly bothers. This may not seem fair until you examine it closer. If a parent said to their child, "Hold my hand and I will stop you falling", but if the child said "No!" and then fell, whose fault was it? God justified Abraham because he trusted Him.

He was not justified by keeping the law, (which hadn't even been introduced at that point). Spiritually Abraham held God's hand.

The Israelites saw all the miracles God performed getting them out of Egypt, plus the opening of the Red Sea for them to cross safely on dry land. The Egyptian army were drowned in it trying to catch them. Incidentally, archaeologists have found a "scrapyard" of Egyptian chariots in the Red Sea where the Israelites crossed.

After all the miracles they had lived through; knowing full well what had happened could not have been done in their own strength; yet they still did not trust the Lord as their father Abraham did.

> "the impossible has already been done, miracles we do straight away."

Stepping out in faith or trust is not attempting what seems possible, but that which is very difficult or indeed impossible, in fact, miraculous. A non-Christian colleague was always saying to me, "the impossible we do straight away, miracles take a little longer", which to me meant his impossible was actually possible. One day I responded, "the impossible has already been done, miracles we do straight away".

Heb 11:3 By faith we understand that the worlds were prepared by the word of God, so that what is seen was not made out of things which are visible.

Faith is the evidence of things not seen. By faith God created everything out of nothing by speaking into the situation. We only have to know God said it, then believe for it to happen.

Plan A goes right back to the beginning when God first created us.

Gen 1:26-28 Then God said, "Let Us make man in Our image, according to Our likeness; and let them rule over the fish of the sea and over the birds of the sky and over the cattle and over all the earth, and over every creeping thing that creeps on the earth." God created man in His own image, in the image of God He created him; male and female He created them. God blessed them; and God said to them, "Be fruitful and multiply, and fill the earth, and subdue it; and rule over the fish of the sea and over the birds of the sky and over every living thing that moves on the earth."

We have seen earlier that He wanted to create us in His own image, and not only that, but for us to have dominion over His creation. This means the need for structure, coordination and authority. Hence the need for a mediator within a group, a priest. So within the family unit there needed to be a priest to communicate. Then, as the family grew and nations were created, so the need for more priests would grow. This would all be within God's kingdom. Christ's message was: "the Kingdom of God has come". His last message to His disciples was "to make disciples of ALL nations" (not just converts), and in the book of Revelation declares them and us to be "a kingdom and priests to our God" who would rule with Him.

So what was the purpose of the robe?

So what was the purpose of the robe? We have seen it was a covering having many symbolic meanings. It was a uniform that signified authority rather like a police uniform. It was a covering of the flesh or body. It acted as a shield protecting the body from the holiness of God's presence. It also protected the priest from the sins of the people as he was making an offering for them. As our High Priest, Christ hung naked on the cross; He took our sin and was exposed to the judgment of God – unprotected.

We will be looking at these spiritual factors of authority and protection in the following chapters.

QUESTIONS

1. What do you see as Plan A?
2. How long historically had Plan A been in God's mind?
3. Give an instance of archaeological evidence that the Egyptians gave chase and lost.
4. How long did Moses look after sheep in the wilderness?
5. What was Christ's last command on Earth?
6. What are disciples described as in the book of Revelation?
7. What was/is the purpose of the robe?

CHAPTER EIGHT
AUTHORITY

Going back before the crucifixion, let us see the authority Jesus demonstrated. If we look at Jesus as a man filled with the Holy Spirit, we can see what is attainable for a believer.

Matt 8:5-10 And when Jesus entered Capernaum, a centurion came to Him, imploring Him, and saying, "Lord, my servant is lying paralyzed at home, fearfully tormented." Jesus said to him, "I will come and heal him." But the centurion said, "Lord, I am not worthy for You to come under my roof, but just say the word, and my servant will be healed. For I also am a man under authority, with soldiers under me; and I say to this one, 'Go!' and he goes, and to another, 'Come!' and he comes, and to my slave, 'Do this!' and he does it." Now when Jesus heard this, He marvelled and said to those who were following, "Truly I say to you, I have not found such great faith with anyone in Israel."

I will come and heal him

Authority is usually recognised. The centurion certainly saw the authority in Jesus and Jesus certainly confirmed it by saying, "I will come and heal him." He didn't say, "I will come and pray for him and hopefully he may be healed." The centurion's observations so impressed Jesus. He obviously recognised that Jesus had an authority that was not of this world and, as we will see in the next section of scripture, others were also astounded by His authority.

Mar 1:22-27 They were amazed at His teaching; for He was teaching them as one having authority, and not as the scribes. Just then there was a man in their synagogue with an unclean spirit; and he cried out, saying, "What business do we have with each other, Jesus of Nazareth? Have You come to destroy us? I know who You are—the Holy One of God!"

And Jesus rebuked him, saying, "Be quiet, and come out of him!" Throwing him into convulsions, the unclean spirit cried out with a loud voice and came out of him. They were all amazed, so that they debated among themselves, saying, "What is this? A new teaching with authority! He commands even the unclean spirits, and they obey Him."

Unclean spirits recognised the authority and obeyed.

Unclean spirits recognised the authority and obeyed. We can easily say, "Yeah, that's fine for Jesus, He's the Son of God. I'm not!" But He says so much in the Bible to show that in the Kingdom of God the same authority has been passed on to us, His disciples, in the Holy Spirit.

Mat 28:18-20 And Jesus came up and spoke to them, saying, "All authority has been given to Me in heaven and on earth. Go therefore and make disciples of all the nations, baptizing them in the name of the Father and the Son and the Holy Spirit, teaching them to observe all that I commanded you; and lo, I am with you always, even to the end of the age."

Mark 16:20 And they went out and preached everywhere, while the Lord worked with them, and confirmed the word by the signs that followed.

All authority has been given to Jesus

All authority has been given to Jesus and He is with us always. That means if we are doing what He has commanded us, He is always there to back us up. Whether it is healing, teaching or casting out unclean spirits, He is there. Spiritually we wear a uniform that spiritual forces recognise. A uniform that gives us, or shows, that we have authority from Jesus.

That is where the Seamless Robe comes in. For instance, we can have money in our wallet and not realise it, but even though we don't realise it that doesn't mean it's not there. But also, we may as well not have it if we don't use it!

Spiritually the robe **IS** on us, spiritually we **ARE** priests to our God. We must do as we are told: make disciples of all nations; heal the sick; teach them about Jesus. As we obey Him, He **WILL** confirm our words with signs following.

QUESTIONS

1. Why was Jesus impressed with the centurion?
2. What impressed the people in the synagogue about Jesus regarding the man with the unclean spirit?
3. Who has ALL authority in heaven and Earth?
4. In spiritual terms what uniform or symbol shows we have authority as priests to other spiritual entities?
5. What were unclean spirits able to recognise?
6. What was the last command Jesus gave to His disciples?
7. How were the disciple's words confirmed and by who?

CHAPTER NINE
YOU, O LORD, ARE A SHIELD ABOUT ME

an invisible force field

Have you ever watched "Atlantis", a story about the ancient city which is a floating spacecraft in an off-world location? Sorry for those of you that can't stand Sci-Fi. When they were being attacked, they raised the shield, which is an invisible force field like a dome over the city, that takes the full blast of the attackers' weapons. It reminds me of David who was a man of war and talks about the protection he experienced from the Lord when in battle.

PSALM 3

A Psalm of David, when he fled from Absalom his son.

O Lord, how my adversaries have increased! Many are rising up against me. Many are saying of my soul, "There is no deliverance for him in God." Selah. But You, O Lord, **are a shield about me,** My glory, and the One who lifts my head. I was crying to the Lord with my voice, And He answered me from His holy mountain. Selah. I lay down and slept; I awoke, for the Lord sustains me. I will not be afraid of ten thousands of people Who have set themselves against me round about. Arise, O Lord; save me, O my God! For You have smitten all my enemies on the cheek; You have shattered the teeth of the wicked. Salvation belongs to the Lord; Your blessing be upon Your people!

Whatever the situation David knew the Lord would protect him. He knew he was one of God's people. Like Abraham, he knew his trust was not in his own righteousness but in God's righteousness.

His enemies were not submitting to, or trusting in God, but trusting in their own power, against a child of God. They had no chance in David's mind. No chance at all! Salvation belongs to the Lord.

Salvation, in Hebrew, is Yeshuah, which is also Hebrew for the name of Jesus. Reading the psalms, it becomes obvious that David knew salvation as Jesus, who is, the Lord. I'm sure David had lots of stories to tell of the Lord's deliverance.

It's the same with those of us who trust in the Lord. There are countless accounts of missionaries going into hostile primitive areas of the world. They have been in their hut at night and natives who came to attack saw "shining" guards with spears standing outside the hut and they were afraid to attack.

Psalm 34:7 The angel of the Lord encamps around those who fear Him,

The Lord's angels distract or divert the enemy. There are many ways we can be clothed for protection. A construction worker will wear a hard hat and metal capped "toetector" boots. Some would say there is no such thing as bad weather, just inadequate clothing. In wet weather we need "wellies" and waterproof clothes. In cold weather we wear extra woollies, etc. In spiritual terms, we need protection against the environment we are spiritually entering. But clothing is more than what we have in our wardrobe.

Psalm 104:1-2 O Lord my God, You are very great; You are clothed with splendour and majesty, Covering Yourself with light as with a cloak.

What were Adam and Eve clothed in before the Fall? If they were created in the image of God, were they also clothed in light? When they sinned, did the splendour, majesty and light they were emitting fade away? Were they like the shining glory of God that faded from Moses when he returned to the people of Israel, or the saints in a stained glass window when the sun sets?

The One who lifts my head

As we saw, David recognised that God was, my glory, and the One who lifts my head. What people wear defines them. It creates an image of what kind of person is beneath the clothes. Adam and Eve, after the fall, covered themselves with leaves to try and conceal their guilt. Was the light shining from Moses and possibly Adam and Eve before the fall, seamless with no weaknesses or joining? Did the seamless robe represent the covering God wore? (Covering Yourself with light as with a cloak.)

Covering Yourself with light as with a cloak

"Oh Lord Jesus we don't know what we will be like, but we know we will be like you, and that is good enough for us."

1Jo 3:2-3 We know that when He appears, we will be like Him, because we will see Him just as He is. And everyone who has this hope fixed on Him purifies himself, just as He is pure.

So fix your hope on Jesus and you will look like Him and be like Him ... and be clothed like Him!

We have considered some of the different points about the Seamless Robe Jesus wore and left at the foot of the cross. Even though we may not grasp the full significance of the Robe, let us in spiritual terms wear it and declare to principalities and powers in heavenly places that we are not ashamed of the gospel.

Nor should we be afraid to wear the Seamless Robe representing God's power, authority and priesthood, worn by a priest after the order of Melchizedek.

In my opening comments I wrote what I felt the Spirit said to me and I will leave you to consider them now: “My church is not a patchwork quilt; this “rag tag bunch”, which you are part of, is a Seamless Robe that I am weaving from top to bottom (starting in Heaven and working its way down to Earth). I have woven you into the robe and anyone that you bring to me I will also weave in, and you can watch as each thread is seamlessly added.”

> I have woven you into the robe

QUESTIONS

1. What has Atlantis to do with Psalm 3?
2. What and who is Yeshuah?
3. What blessing is promised in Psalm 34:7?
4. What is God clothed in according to Psalm 104?
5. How does what we wear define us?
6. If our hope is in Jesus what will we be like when He returns?
7. In what way have the discussions on Seamless Robe impacted you?

ABOUT THE AUTHOR

Brian Johnson is an active member of Coton Green Church, holding a variety of roles. For a number of years, he has been involved in prison ministry bringing the message of hope to many experiencing hopelessness.

FOR MORE INFORMATION

For enquiries, please write to:
PRISON MINISTRIES
The Coton Centre
Comberford Road
Tamworth
Staffordshire
B79 9AA

FOR MORE ON THE SEAMLESS ROBE AND OTHER BOOKS

For further copies, contact Refreshment at their website:

RETREAT REJOICE RESPOND RESOURCE
REFRESHMENT
www.refreshment.org.uk
Registered Charity - 1153542